Thank you to the generous team who gave their time and talents to make this book possible:

Author
Jekap Omod with Jane Kurtz

Illustrator
Jordy Farrell

Creative directors
**Caroline Kurtz, Jane Kurtz,
and Kenny Rasmussen**

Translator
Abdi Mohamed Hassen

Editors
**Mastewal Abera and
Woubeshet Ayenew**

Inclusivity Consultant
Elizabeth Spor Taylor

Designer
Beth Crow

Ready Set Go Books, an Open Hearts Big Dreams Project
Copyright © 2023 Ready Set Go Books

ISBN: 979-8392329861
Library of Congress Control Number: 2023916936

Publication Date: 9/20/2023

The Lonely Nile Perch

Kaluunkii kalidiis Noolaa.

English and Somali

One day, visitors came to the banks of our river. We were afraid because they did not look like anyone we had seen before.

Maalin maalmaha kamid ah ayey dad dal xiisayaal ahi yimaadeen wabiga.markaanu aragnay waanu ka cabsanaynay sabatoo ah horay umaanaan arrag dad iyagoo kale ah.

The storyteller told them to come sit down. "Listen to this story," she said.

Gabadhii sheekada nooga sheekaynaysay ayaa nagu tidhi kaalaya soo fadhiista oo sheekada dhagaysta.

The king of the Openo River was a
giant Nile perch. He felt important
but he was also very lonely.

Waxaa wabiga ku noolaa kaluun
aad u wayn.wuxuu aaminsan yahay
inuu muhiim yahay laakin wuxuu
ahaa mid kaligii ah.

One day, the Nile perch spotted a hippopotamus. "Hello," he said. "How are you? My name is Nile Perch, but you can call me..."

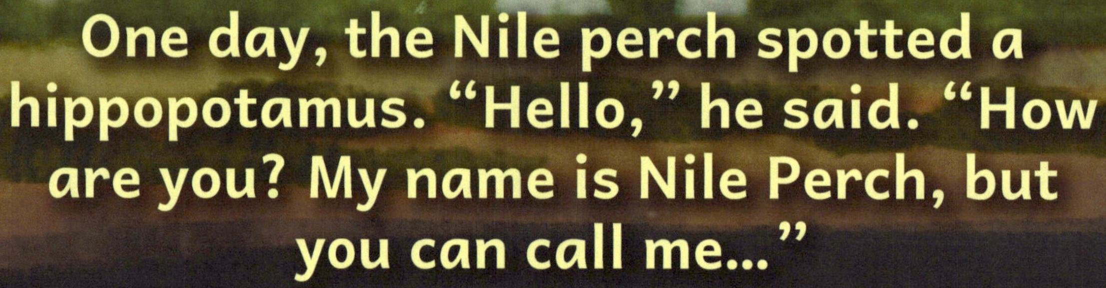

Maalin maalmaha kamid ayuu kaluunkii la kulmay jeer wayn. wuxuuna ku yidhi iiwaran?magacaygu waa Nile Perch balse waxaad iigu yeedhi kartaa---

Oops. The hippopotamus was gone.

Jeertii way ka tagtay

The Nile perch swam on.
He spotted a smallmouth
electric catfish.
"Hello," he said. "How are
you? My name is Nile Perch,
but you can call me..."

Wuxuu kaluunkii kusii
dabaashay wabiga Nile.
wuxuu arkay kaluun yar.
wuxuuna ku yidhi iiwaran
seetahay?magacaygu waa
Nile Perch waxaa kalood iigu
yeedhi kartaa------

Oops. The smallmouth electric catfish was gone.

Kaluunkii yaraa wuu ka cararay markuu arkay.

The Nile perch swam on sadly. He spotted
a puffer fish. Before the fish could swim
away, the Nile perch quickly asked, "Why
is everyone is afraid of me?"

Kaluunkii waynaa isagoo murugoonaya
ayuu biyihii wabiga sii dhax qaaday. Waxa
uu arkay kalluun yar oo kale. Intuusan
kaluunkii yaraa ka cararin ayaa
wuxuu si degdeg ah u waydiiyay,
"Maxay dadka oo dhammi
iiga baqayaan?"

The puffer fish began to shake. "Everyone is afraid of you because you do not look like anyone else. You might bite us with your big teeth."

Kaluunkii yaraa ayaa is ruxay.wuxuuna ugu jawaabay dadkoo dhani way kaa baqayaan sabatoo ah qofna uma ekid adigu .waxaana suuragal ah inaad ilkahaaga dhaadheer nagu qaniinto.

The Nile perch thought and thought. "So that's why I'm alone," he said to himself. "At least the crocodile won't be afraid of me."

Kaluunkii waynaa ee Nile perch aad ayuu u fikiray. wuxuuna naftiisii ka dhaadhiciyey inay arrintaas tahay sababta uu kalidiis u yahay.laakiin waxaa suuragal ah inuusan yaxaasku iga baqin ayuu yidhi.

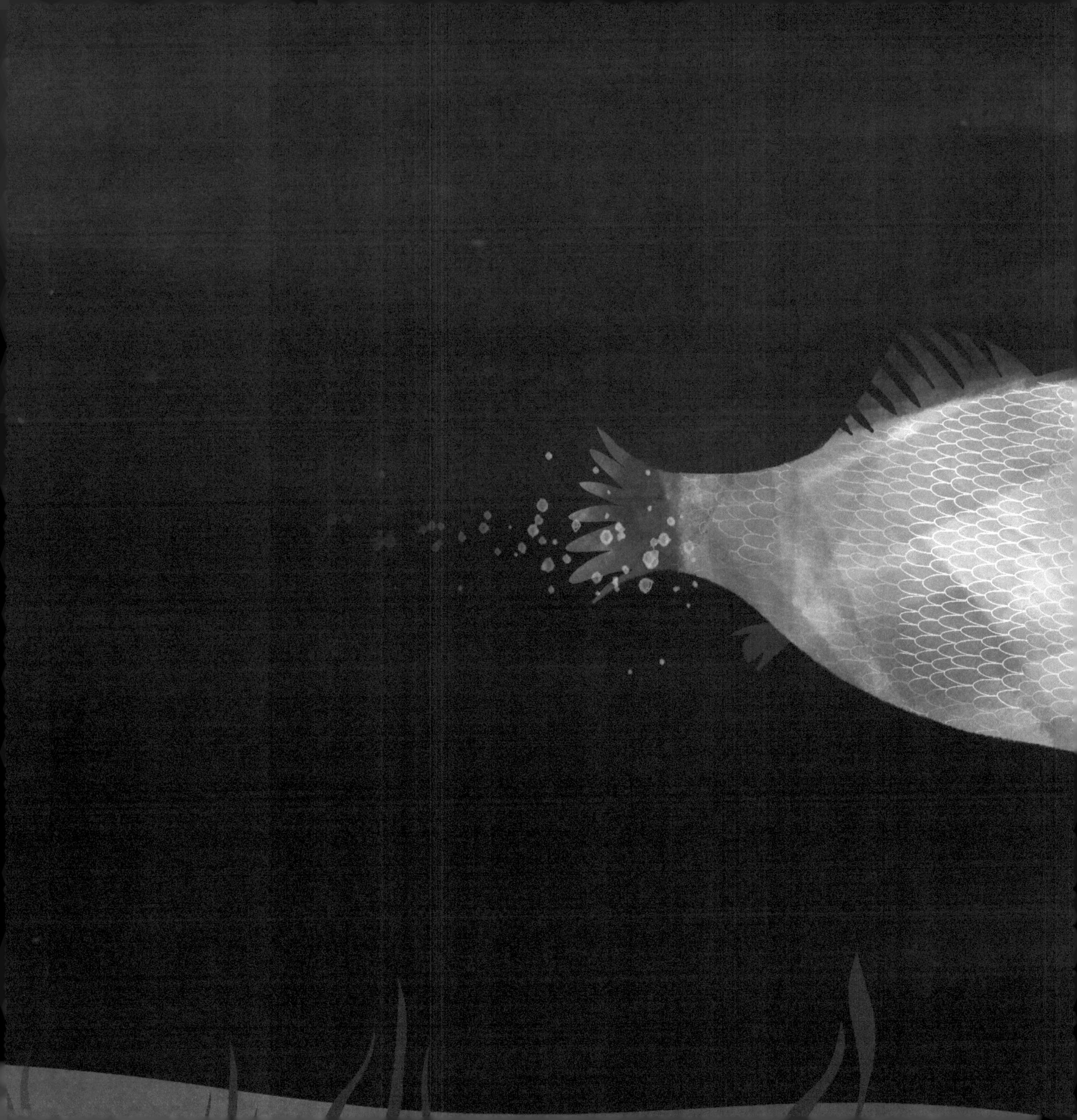

But the crocodile was afraid.

Balse laakiin yaxaaskiina wuu ka cabsaday.

"Wait," the Nile perch called. "You don't have to be afraid of me. I don't even have teeth."

kaluunkii waynaa ee Nile Perch ayaa yaxaaskii ku yidhi sug ha cararin.inaad iga cabsato ma aha. xiitaa wax ilka ah ma lihi anigu.

"I don't believe you," the crocodile said. "Prove it."

Yaxaaskii ayaa ugu jawaabay
kuma aaminayo anigu

The Nile perch opened his
mouth into a wide smile.

Kadib kaluunkii waynaa ayaa isagoo
qoslaya afka kala qaaday.

The crocodile swam closer to get
a better look. He couldn't believe
what he was seeing.

"Follow me," he said. "We can play
hide and seek."

Yaxaaskii ayaa usoo dhawaaday kaluunkii si
uu si fiican u eego. yaxaasikii wuu rumaysan
waayey wuxuu arkay.

Kaluunkii ayaa yaxaaskii ku yidhi Kaalay
isoo raac aan dhuumaalaysanee.

They swam and swam. The Nile
perch said, "We have come a long
way. I don't know this place."

"Don't worry," The crocodile said.
"I know the way home."

Kadib markay in badan dabaasheen
kaluunkii waynaa ayaa yaxaaskii ku
yidhi "in badan Ayaan soo soconay".
meeshana ma aha meel aan garanaayo.

Yaxaaskii ayaa ug jawaabay "waxba
haka baqin aniga ayaa garanaaya jidkii
guriga aadayee".

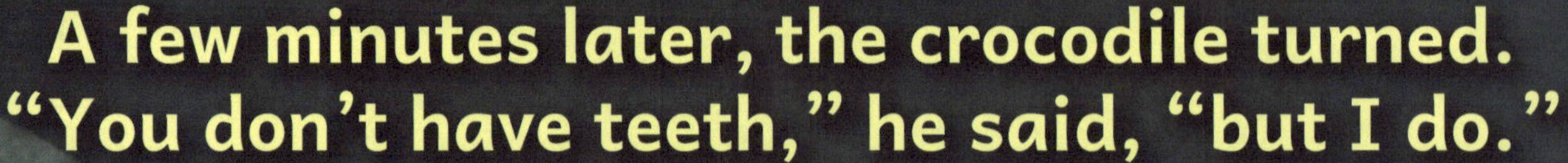

A few minutes later, the crocodile turned.
"You don't have teeth," he said, "but I do."

Daqiiqado kadib yaxaaskii ayaa intuu
kaluunkii ku soo jeedsaday ku yidhi
"adigu ilko malihid
laakiin anigu ilko
ayaan leeyahay".

The Nile perch swam away as fast as he could go.

Kaluunkii dib ayuu si xawli ah ugu
cararay intuu awoodayey.

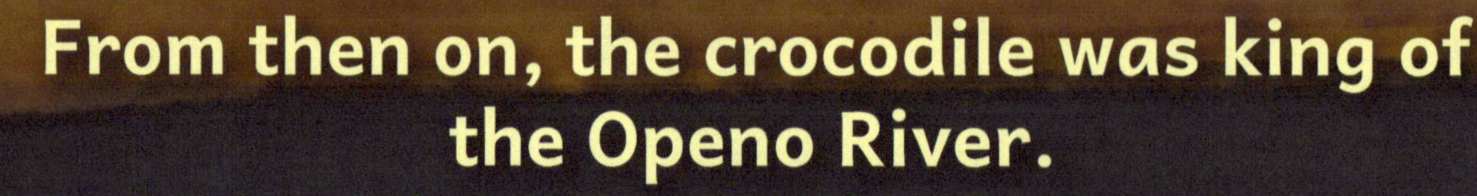

From then on, the crocodile was king of
the Openo River.

Maalintaas intii ka dadanbaysay yaxaaska
ayaa noqday Boqorkii wabiga Nile.

But the Nile perch went to the other animals. "I may be different," he said, "but if you play with me, you'll see that you don't need to be afraid."

Kaluunkii waynaana wuxuu ku laabtay la noolaanshaha xayawaankii kale wuxuuna ku yidhi 'waa suuragal inaan idinka duwanahay balse laakiin waan wada ciyaari karnaa idnkoon iga baqaynin".

"You see?" the storyteller said. "It isn't fair to judge people before we know them."

Dulucda sheekadu waa inaan dadka waxaysan ahayn lagu qiimaynin inaadan baranin ka hor,

We all knew what to do next.
It was time to play.

Hada dhamaanteen waynu garanaynaa waxaan
samaynayno.waana wakhtigaan ciyaari lahayn
ee ina mariya aan ciyaarnee.

About The Story

For hundreds of years, the Anywaa people (often called Anuak by those outside the community), have lived in the Gambella Region in southwest Ethiopia, sharing oral stories remembered from childhood. The Lonely Nile Perch is an adaptation of one such folktale, passed down from generation to generation. Jane Kurtz and Elizabeth Taylor had many conversations with Jekap Omod about retelling the story for a wider audience—in writing with illustrations.

The giant Nile perch represented in the story, is a species that lives in the waters of the Openo River. The river is life to the Anywaa community of farmers, fishermen, mothers, elders, hunters, and herdsmen. Their diet consists mainly of sorghum flour, maize, fish meat, and fowl.

The Anywaa have a social structure based on family and community life. There are 250,000 to 300,000 members, now living throughout the world. Their mother tongue Dha-anywaa is spoken throughout the region and can be heard each Sunday in their Christian churches. Beads are an important symbol in the culture. Many traditional customs are based on bead giving.

Jekap Omod writes, "Throughout time, the Anuak people have faced kidnapping, invasion, killing, and land grabbing. While a peaceful and welcoming population of people, they are known to be a bit suspicious of strangers as a direct result of historical hardships. This suspicious nature has helped them keep their culture and customs alive."

*Image Source: https://www.theguardian.com/environment/2019/
may/27/secretive-traders-netting-chinese-delicacy-leave-nile-perch-
under-threat*

Nile perch facts:

Large mouthed fish
Greenish brownish in colour on top and silvery below
Six feet (1.8 meters) long
Weighs 300 pounds (140 kg)
Lives in freshwater
Provides food security in East Africa
Invasive (harmful) species

About The Author

Jekap Omod was born and raised in Gambella, Ethiopia. He is an Anuak also known as Anywaa or Anyuak, a minority ethnic group living at the border of Ethiopia and South Sudan. Jekap is a genocide survivor and grew up with no access to a better education. Growing up in Ethiopia, Jekap only had access to school-textbooks provided by the government. He never experienced what it is like to have bedtime stories, nor did he have access to children's books. The only books he had available in his mother tongue were the New Testament Bible, and few samples from the Old Testament. In 2014, Jekap moved to the United States with his family and took advantage of the opportunities he had for school. He studied Neuroscience at the University of Minnesota. As a literacy advocate, Jekap joined the Open Hearts Big Dreams and translated the "Anuak and English" children's books for the first time in the Anuak (Anywaa) history.

Here are the two goals Jekap is working on to achieve through the help of OHBD organization:

1. PRESERVING the Anuak language and culture abroad and back home in Gambella through literacy. Jekap believes that the Anuak children living in the United States and other western countries need to keep their mother tongue and their culture.

2. Improving and increasing the REPRESENTATION of Anuak literacy in Ethiopia. Growing up with no access to books or reading books in his mother tongue, Jekap felt like his native language was underrepresented, unvalued, and lesser compared to Amharic or English, which were the most common languages in his region's schools. Jekap believes that representation in literacy would boost and enhance the willingness to read, particularly for the children. He also believes that children should have access to books that represent them as a people and show their culture.

About the Illustrator

Jordy Farrell is a designer and illustrator currently living in Portland, OR. He works at LAIKA and is a children's book illustrator on the side. After earning a BFA in Fine Arts from Thiel College, he moved to San Francisco and attended the Academy of Art University, where he earned his MFA in Illustration, focusing in children's books and visual development.

About Michael Carr's Legacy Project

Disability does not define a life. Mike Carr clearly demonstrated that his life was not defined by his disability. Although Mike was paralyzed at a young age, he still enjoyed a successful career with a high-tech company in Seattle where both his technical skills and leadership were highly valued. Mike was a role model to so many of those he worked with and those who came to know him. He was a strong advocate for the power of inclusion and equal opportunity for individuals with disabilities. The legacy project in his name was created to provide opportunities for children with disabilities in Ethiopia, the birth country of one of his sons. Children with disabilities there do not lack talent or drive. What they too often lack, however, are the tools needed to develop these talents and to apply that drive.

Education remains the key to providing those tools. Unfortunately, educational opportunities for children with disabilities in Ethiopia are rare or in some cases, non-existent. The goal of the legacy project is to increase awareness of the educational disparities of Ethiopian children with disabilities and to increase educational opportunities for these children so they can become the role models of the future that Mike Carr was during his lifetime. Getting to see themselves in our OHBD-RSG is an important step to making this possible.

About Open Hearts Big Dreams

Open Hearts Big Dreams Fund (OHBD) was founded by Ellenore Angelidis, inspired by her Ethiopian born daughter, Leyla Marie Fasika; both are key volunteers. OHBD is a United State 501(c)(3) not-for-profit organization that believes the chance to dream big dreams should not depend on where in the world you are born. Our mission is "Inspiring and empowering youth (K-14) to reimagine their futures by providing literacy, STEAM, and leadership opportunities."

OHBD harnesses the power of collaboration. We are made up of a small number of part-time paid staff and a large number of highly motivated volunteers with advanced skills, including artistic, editorial, translation, and high-tech expertise in Ethiopia, the Diaspora and globally. Our culture of innovation means we act fast on new ideas. Since 2017, we've produced more than 700 bilingual, culturally appropriate early reader titles and a number of STEM and Model programs to increase literacy, inclusion, and leadership.

In Ethiopia, for Ethiopia; OHBD is based in the U.S. but we are committed to working with local content creators and to producing quality books in Ethiopia. Local opportunities and production builds local knowledge and capacity.

About OHBD Ready Set Go Books

Reading has the power to change lives, but many children and adults in Ethiopia cannot read. One reason is that Ethiopia doesn't have enough books in local languages to give people a chance to practice reading. Ready Set Go books wants to close that gap and open a world of ideas and possibilities for kids and their communities.

When you buy an OHBD-RSG book, you provide critical funding to create and distribute more books.

Learn more at: http://openheartsbigdreams.org/book-project/ or find all our books at: https://ohbd-rsgbooks.com

About The Inclusivity Consultant

Elizabeth Spor Taylor is an international literacy specialist with an expertise in primary grades literacy for ESL and first language English learners. She has worked to improve literacy throughout Ethiopia by writing and editing English textbooks and learning materials, authoring and illustrating Ready Set Go books and coaching Ethiopian children's book authors.

OHBD Proudly Prints in Ethiopia

OHBD developed our own local printing capacity and have a number of our books available to pick up in Addis. They are available for bulk purchase and we regularly donate to schools, libraries and local organizations serving kids. Please contact us at ellenore@openheartsbigdreams.org if interested in samples or ordering.

So far, we have printed and distributed (with collaborating organizations) hundreds of thousands of copies of our books in numerous languages in country.

Our goal is to get these books to all elementary students across Ethiopia.

About the Language

Somali is an Afroasiatic language belonging to the Cushitic branch. Somali is spoken in Somalia, Somaliland, Djibouti, Ethiopia and Kenya. It is used as an adoptive language by a few neighboring ethnic groups and individuals. Somali was not written until the Osmanya alphabet was developed in 1920. The Latin alphabet was adopted in 1972.

About the Translation

Abdi Mohamed Hassen was born in 1987 in Sagag Distinct of Nogob Zone of the Somali Regional State. He completed primary school in Kebribayah and secondary school in Jigjiga. Abdi graduated from Addis Ababa University with BA Degree in Foreign Language and Literature(English). He also graduated MA or second degree of Educational Planning and Management at Jigjiga University. For the last 10 years has worked in the Somali Regional Education Bureau.